THE
FALL
OF
THE
INCAS

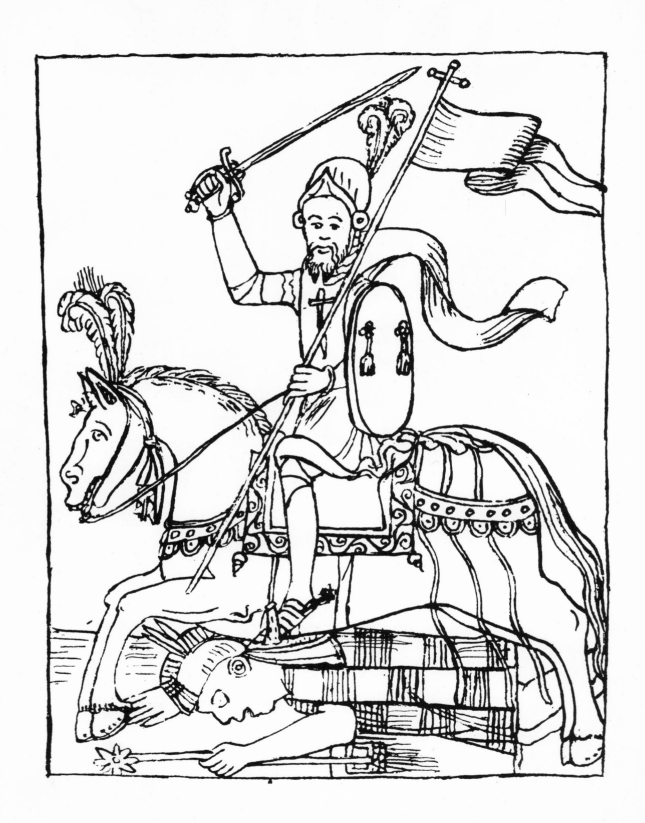

THE
FALL
OF
THE
INCAS

SHIRLEY GLUBOK

Designed by Gerard Nook

THE MACMILLAN COMPANY, NEW YORK • COLLIER-MACMILLAN LIMITED, LONDON

The author gratefully acknowledges the cooperation of:
ALLAN D. CHAPMAN, Librarian, The Museum of Primitive Art
MATTHEW SHIPMAN
MARILYN ALLEN
And especially the kind assistance of:
ALFRED H. TAMARIN

Other books by Shirley Glubok:

THE ART OF ANCIENT EGYPT

THE ART OF LANDS IN THE BIBLE

THE ART OF ANCIENT GREECE

THE ART OF THE NORTH AMERICAN INDIAN

THE ART OF THE ESKIMO

THE ART OF ANCIENT ROME

THE ART OF AFRICA

ART AND ARCHAEOLOGY

THE ART OF ANCIENT PERU

THE ART OF THE ETRUSCANS

The Fall of the Incas is abridged and adapted from *Relation of the Discovery and Conquest of
the Kingdoms of Peru* by Pedro Pizarro, translated by Philip Ainsworth Means, published by
The Cortez Society, and from *Royal Commentaries of the Incas* by the Inca Garcilaso de la Vega,
translated and edited by Clements R. Markham, published by the Hakluyt Society.

People who live during momentous times and take part in great events often write accounts of personal experiences which are very exciting and colorful.

This story of the rise and fall of the Inca Empire is based on the works of two such writers. One of them was the Inca Garcilaso de la Vega. His father was a Spaniard who fought alongside Francisco Pizarro, the conquerer of Peru. His mother was an Inca princess, a first cousin to the ruling kings of Peru. Garcilaso was born in 1539, just six years after the fall of the Incas. At the age of twenty he left the New World, never to return. As an old man, living in Spain, he wrote for his father's people an explanation of the history and traditions of his mother's people. He searched his own memory, recalled stories related by his mother's family, and sought out other accounts from old friends.

Garcilaso's *Royal Commentaries of the Incas* begins with the pre-Empire rulers—some real, some legendary. Their story makes up the first part of this book. The second part covers the period of the Inca Empire, which began around 1438 and lasted only a little over ninety years.

The stories are handed down from memory, so some are out of sequence; and there are other inaccuracies. For instance, Garcilaso attributes the stirring defense of Cuzco to Viracocha Inca. Later historians say the episode's hero was really Viracocha's son, Pachacútec, usually considered the founder of the empire. But because of his charm in storytelling, his vivid pride in his own past, and the value of his work as an almost first-hand account, Garcilaso's is a document of literary and historical importance.

Pedro Pizarro, a cousin of the famous conquistador, was, when a young man, a member of the conquering expedition—a Spanish victor. His eyewitness account of the conquest, written in his old age, makes up the third section of this book.

Garcilaso filled his *Commentaries* with descriptions of Inca life, customs, laws, beliefs, and rules of conduct. These accounts are grouped together in the fourth section, after the Pizarro narrative of the fall of the Incas.

The drawings in this book are by Felipe Huaman Poma de Ayala, an Indian who wrote and illustrated his own book, *"Nueva y Buen Gobierno Chronica."*

Shirley Glubok

PART I

From Garcilaso de la Vega

Having to treat of the New World, especially the kingdoms and provinces of the empire called Peru, I shall tell about the origins of the Incas, kings of Peru, and of their succession, conquests, and laws. I heard many things that happened in my country, Peru, from my Spanish father and his contemporaries. They had met many of the Spaniards who were the first discoverers and conquerors of the New World, and from them had heard a full account of events.

As we are about to treat of Peru, it seems to me best also to relate what I often heard from my mother and her brothers, uncles, and other relations. My mother, an Inca princess, resided in Cuzco, and almost every week some relations came to visit her. The usual subject of their conversation was the origins of the Inca kings, their majesty, and the grandeur of their empire.

One day, when I was sixteen or seventeen years old, I said to the most aged of the family, "Inca, my uncle, who was the first of our Inca kings? What beginning had our history?"

My uncle said, "Nephew, I will tell you with great pleasure and you should preserve what I say in your heart.

"Our father the Sun placed his two children on Lake Titicaca. He told them they might go where they pleased but that they were to thrust a scepter of gold into the ground at every place where they stopped to eat or sleep. In that place where, by one blow, the gold scepter should disappear, he told them to establish their court.

"The children of the Sun set out and traveled northward. Wherever they stopped they thrust the golden scepter into the earth, but it never sank in. Then on a hill south of Cuzco the scepter buried itself in the ground and was

never seen again. The children called the Indians of the area together and they assembled in great numbers, both men and women. In this manner our imperial city began to be settled. As you know, we have built a temple on the spot where the golden scepter sank into the earth.

"These two were our first rulers, who appeared in the first ages of the world, and from them we are all descended. Our first Inca was called Manco Cápac and our first Coya, or queen, Mama Ocllo Huaco.

"And that I may not make you weep, I have not related the story with tears of blood, at seeing that our royal line is ended and our empire lost."

Now that we have laid the foundation stone of our history (although it be legendary), it will be well to pass on. I was born eight years after the Spaniards conquered my country. I had the opportunity of seeing with my own eyes a great many of the Incas' customs and festivals, which were celebrated even until I was twelve or thirteen years of age.

In addition, as soon as I resolved to write this history, I wrote to my old schoolfellows, asking each to send me an account of the Inca conquest in his province; for each province has its own history, with its own recorded annals and traditions.

The Inca Manco Cápac established his people in villages, taught them to cultivate the land, to build houses, to construct channels for irrigation, and to do all the other things necessary for human life. He instructed them in the ways of polite and brotherly companionship. He directed that flocks of llamas be collected, so that his people might be clothed with wool. They were also taught to make shoes.

Manco Cápac built a temple where his subjects might make sacrifices to the Sun, who caused their crops to grow and their flocks to multiply. He ordered the Indians to worship the Sun as a god because of its beauty and splendor.

The Indians also considered Manco Cápac and Mama Ocllo Huaco to be gods, for they believed that these two were the Sun's children, who had come down from Heaven.

In addition, the Indians worshiped Pachacámac as the supreme god who created Heaven and the earth. Pachacámac means "he who gives animation to the universe."

The Inca Manco Cápac

Mama Ocllo Huaco

Manco Cápac wore a tress of hair one finger in width, and a headdress of many colors. He was shaven with stone razors. His ears were bored, and the ornaments inserted in them were like stoppers.

The first privilege that Manco Cápac granted his subjects was to permit them to imitate him in wearing a headdress, but their headdresses were to be of one color only: black. The people were also permitted to have their heads shaven, but in fashions differing from the Inca. After several years, he allowed his subjects to bore their ears, but the holes could not be as large as those of the Inca.

Because of this custom of boring their ears, the Spaniards called the Indians *Orejones*, which means "long-eared men."

The Inca Manco Cápac reserved one of his many badges for himself and his descendants. This was a red fringe which he wore across his forehead. The Prince, his heir apparent, wore a smaller yellow fringe.

Our first Inca reigned many years. Finally, when he grew old, he ordered his chiefs, called *Curacas*, to assemble, and he said to them that he would soon return to rest with his father the Sun. As he had to depart, he wished to give them his royal name, and he decreed that they and their descendants should forever be called Incas. Manco Cápac left as his heir his eldest son Sinchi Roca.

Sinchi is an adjective meaning "valiant." Sinchi Roca was brave and very strong. He had the advantage of all persons of his time in wrestling, running, leaping, throwing a stone or lance, and in every feat of strength.

He married his eldest sister, in imitation of his father and of the Sun who had married the Moon, for in those times it was believed that the Moon was the sister and wife of the Sun.

It is not known how long Sinchi Roca reigned. He left his son Lloque Yupanqui as his successor. *Lloque* means "left-handed." The name Yupanqui was given this Inca for his virtuous actions.

After taking possession of his kingdom, Lloque Yupanqui turned his attention to conquest. To conceal his ambitions, he told everyone that his acts were commanded by the Sun. He assembled six or seven thousand men of war, and crossed his own frontier into a great province called Cana. He sent messages to the inhabitants of the province demanding that they surrender. They submitted and agreed to obey the Inca and keep his laws and customs.

The Inca Sinchi Roca

The Inca Lloque Yupanqui

Lloque Yupanqui marched onward until he reached Ayaviri, where the natives refused to submit. They preferred to die in defending their liberty. They came forth to fight, obliging the Incas to use their arms. Lloque Yupanqui tried to avoid injuring the enemy as much as possible. He laid siege to the Ayaviris and pressed them on all sides, so that they were straitened for want of food.

When Inca reinforcements arrived, the Ayaviris thought it time to give in.

After a few years, Lloque Yupanqui set out with some troops for the district of Collasuyu, and demanded that the Collas submit to his forces. The Collas took counsel and replied that they were well satisfied to become vassals of the Inca and to worship the Sun.

Seeing his success, Lloque Yupanqui then sent similar messages to all the neighboring tribes, as far as the Desaguardero, the river that drains the great Lake Titicaca. All these tribes agreed to become vassals.

After this expedition, the Inca engaged in visiting his kingdom and extending cultivation of the land. He ordered the construction of irrigation channels, bridges, and roads. The Incas used their considerable knowledge of geometry in building these works, making measurements, and marking boundaries by means of cords and small stones.

From north to south, Lloque Yupanqui had added more than 120 miles of land to his kingdom and from east to west more than sixty miles. His holdings now reached to the foot of the snow-capped range of mountains that divides the *llanos* or sandy deserts of the coast from the *sierra* country inland.

When the Inca felt that death was approaching he called his sons, among them his heir Maita Cápac, and informed them that the Sun had called him to rest from his labors.

Lloque Yupanqui was mourned with great sorrow, for he was much loved. As was the custom when a king died, the Indians closed the room where he had slept, and it was looked upon as a sacred place which no one was ever again to enter.

The Inca's favorite servants and most beloved wives were buried alive with him or killed, as the Indians believed that they had to serve their lord in the next world. The King's jewels and clothes and all his other possessions were also buried with him, so that he could use them in the life to come.

After performing the burial rites for his father, Maita Cápac solemnly

The Inca Maita Cápac

took possession of his kingdom and visited his realms. Upon his return he ordered an army collected, and marched to the Desaguardero. He ferried his troops across the river on great rafts of balsa wood.

The villages on the other side of the river readily surrendered to the Incas. Among the places that submitted was Tiahuanaco, a town with wonderful statues and buildings. In one part of the town there are two giant stone figures wearing long robes. These figures are well worn by the hand of time which proves their great antiquity. In other parts there are buildings with great doorways of masonry, some made out of a single stone.

The Indians say that these monuments were constructed by some unknown people before the time of the Incas, and they believe that they were all erected in a single night.

Having passed three years in these expeditions, Maita Cápac went back to Cuzco, where he was welcomed with great festivities.

The Inca soon assembled troops for new conquests.

As he wished to cross the river Apurímac, Maita Cápac ordered the construction of a rope bridge.

This bridge, the first and longest of all such bridges, is about two hundred paces across and sways perilously in the mountain winds. I have seen many Spaniards refuse to get off their horses to cross it, and some go over it at a gallop to show that they are not afraid.

Maita Cápac crossed this bridge with his troops and marched to the province of Cuntisuyu. The people of this province were so astonished at the marvelous bridge that they desired the Inca to be their lord. For the Indians of Peru were so simple that anyone who invented a new thing was readily recognized by them as a god. (It was for this reason that later, when the Indians saw the Spaniards riding on the backs of such ferocious animals as horses appeared to be, and beheld them with guns, killing people at a distance of two or three hundred paces, they looked upon such men as gods and submitted with little opposition.)

After a few days, Maita Cápac marched a distance of sixteen leagues and encountered a formidable swamp, which checked the progress of his army. He had a causeway of stones constructed. The Inca himself worked on the causeway, and it was finished in a few days. The Indians still hold it in veneration.

Maita Cápac passed over the swamp with his army and entered a province called Allca. After conquering this nation, he passed onward to other great provinces and subdued them all. He then marched back to Cuzco where his return was celebrated by dances and songs.

Like his ancestors, Maita Cápac is said to have ruled for thirty years, a little more or less. He died full of honor, gained both in peace and in war, and left as his heir his eldest son Cápac Yupanqui.

The Inca Cápac Yupanqui took the emblem of power, the red fringe, and set out to visit his dominions, the first act of every new king upon his accession. This journey was made so that the king might be known and loved by his vassals, and in order to prevent the governors, judges, and other ministers of the various provinces from becoming careless or tyrannical.

After this inspection, Cápac Yupanqui marched westward with a large body of troops and conquered several provinces.

Next he made an expedition to Lake Paria, the extreme limit of his father's conquests in that direction, and reduced the surrounding countryside to obedience.

Because he intended to proceed with the subjugation of other lands, Cápac Yupanqui ordered the construction of a second bridge over the Desaguardero. The bridge was made of reeds, twisted fibers, and other materials and floated on the water like a chain of boats. It was fourteen feet wide, more than a yard high, and about 150 paces in length.

As soon as the bridge was finished Cápac Yupanqui crossed over it and set out with the Prince his heir to conquer the most distant nations. The Prince sent the usual messages to the inhabitants of these places demanding that they surrender.

Nearly all these nations submitted to the Incas, saying that they considered it an auspicious thing to worship the Sun, and to have the Inca, his child, as their lord.

After this last expedition, Cápac Yupanqui remained at his court in Cuzco, attending to the government of his kingdom, which now extended for more than 540 miles. In this period of quiet and rest he died. He left his eldest son Inca Roca as his successor.

The Inca Roca, whose name means "a prudent prince of mature judgment,"

The Inca Cápac Yupanqui

The Inca Roca and his son

took the red fringe and toured his dominions. He then assembled an army, as he wished to continue the conquests to the north.

He had another bridge built over the river Apurímac, which he crossed with his troops, advancing to the great kingdom of Antahuailla.

The inhabitants of this province were rich and very warlike. They were called Chancas and boasted that they were descended from a lion.

The Chancas submitted to the yoke of the Inca more through fear of his arms than for love of his laws and government. They sent word that they would meekly accept Inca Roca as their lord, and obey his ordinances. But they did not lose the rancor of their hearts, as we shall presently see.

After some years during which Inca Roca remained at peace, he collected thirty thousand soldiers, a larger force than had ever before been brought together by any of his predecessors. The Inca marched as far as the place now called the city of La Plata.

After a successful campaign, he returned to Cuzco and devoted his time to the administration of his empire. When he died he had not degenerated in any respect from the virtues of his ancestors.

On the death of King Inca Roca, his son Yáhuar Huácac assumed the crown. The name Yáhuar Huácac means "he who weeps blood." Some Indians relate that this Inca wept blood when he was a child of three or four. Others declare that he was born weeping blood. Believing so much in omens, the Indians foresaw some great misfortune for him. Yáhuar Huácac hoped that if he did nothing to anger his father the Sun he would not suffer a misfortune, as the soothsayers had threatened. He adorned his provinces with magnificent buildings, gave presents to his vassals, and treated his subjects with greater kindness than had been the custom with any of the Incas who had ruled before him.

All this was a sign of fear, but in order not to appear a coward among his people, Yáhuar Huácac resolved to send an army of twenty thousand warriors southwest of Cuzco to Arequipa and the coast beyond, where a large, sparsely peopled territory had been left unconquered.

The Inca did not dare to take the field in person. Instead he appointed his brother captain-general of the army.

The conquest was completed with such success and dispatch that Yáhuar Huácac resolved to lead another campaign himself. Although he kept his resolu-

tion and this expedition was also successful, the Inca conducted it with much hesitation and fear.

Yáhuar Huácac's worry and anxiety were increased by cares within his household, caused by the character of his eldest son and heir. The Prince had shown a bad disposition from childhood: ill-treating the boys of his own age, and displaying a tendency to be harsh and cruel. The Inca tried to correct his son, but to no avail. At last he determined to disgrace his son by banishing him from the royal presence. If this punishment did not cure the Prince, the King planned to disinherit him and select one of his other sons as his heir. The Prince was therefore sent to a wilderness called Chita, a little more than three miles east of Cuzco. There were large flocks belonging to the Sun on the plains there, and the Prince was ordered to live with the shepherds who had charge of them.

After banishing his son, Yáhuar Huácac gave up all ideas of further wars and conquests and devoted himself to the government of his kingdom.

One day, three years later, the exiled Prince returned to the house of his father and sent word that he was bound to deliver a certain message. The Inca replied in great wrath that the Prince was to return to his flocks at once unless he wished to be punished with death. The Prince answered that he had not come to break his father's commandment but to obey another Inca as great as the King, who had sent him.

Yáhuar Huácac, hearing the assertion that there was another lord as great as himself, ordered his son to enter that he might learn what nonsense this was. As soon as he had been brought before his father, the Prince said, "O sole Lord, when I was lying down at noon today (I cannot say whether I was asleep or awake) a strange man stood before me. He said to me: 'Nephew, I am a child of the Sun and brother of the Inca Manco Cápac, the first of your ancestors. I am called Viracocha Inca. I come to give you a warning that you may deliver to the Inca Yáhuar Huácac my brother. The subject province of Chinchasuyu is in rebellion, and a great multitude has assembled to drive him from his throne. Go, therefore, and tell him to prepare himself and to take all necessary steps to avert this danger. As for you, whatever difficulty you may encounter, fear not, for I will not fail you. Therefore, do not hesitate to undertake any adventure if it adds to the glory of your empire, for I will always be at your side.' Having said these words, the Inca Viracocha disappeared.

The Inca Yáhuar Huácac

"Then I set out to deliver his message to you."

The Inca Yáhuar Huácac was so enraged against his son that he would not believe his story. He ordered him to return to Chita at once and not to leave it again. So the Prince went back to tend his flocks; but the brothers and uncles of the Inca, being superstitious and believers in omens, and especially in dreams, received what the Prince had said in another spirit. They argued that the words of the Prince should be examined one by one, that sacrifices to the Sun should be made, and oracles consulted to see whether what they foretold was good or evil. But the Inca Yáhuar Huácac insisted that no notice should be taken of the speech of a madman like his son.

Three months after the dream of the Prince Viracocha Inca (for so he was called by his people from that time forward), an uncertain rumor came concerning rebellion in the province of Chinchasuyu, but Yáhuar Huácac disregarded it. A few days later the same news again reached him. A third notice of the rebellion stated that the nations called Chanca and others had slain the royal governors and ministers in their areas, and were marching to the capital with an army of more than forty thousand warriors.

These nations, seeing that Yáhuar Huácac was not warlike and that he was intimidated by the evil omens of his name, "he who weeps blood," felt the time was favorable for them to show their hatred for the government of the Incas. They expected that they would easily conquer Yáhuar Huácac because of the speed with which they could move and because of the lack of preparation on his part.

Yáhuar Huácac was confused by the news that the enemy was approaching; for no province had rebelled from the time of the first Inca Manco Cápac. Passion had blinded Yáhuar Huácac's understanding, and now he was unprepared, and had no time to assemble his men either to advance against the enemy or to garrison Cuzco. Instead of waiting until help could come, it seemed better to fall back before the rebels and retire toward Collasuyu. He thus retreated and halted fifteen miles south of Cuzco to obtain news of the movement of the rebels.

Cuzco, deserted by its king, was in confusion. There was no captain or chief who dared give orders to defend it. All were seeking safety in flight. Some of the fugitives went to Prince Viracocha and gave him news of the rebellion and

told him how the King his father had retreated. The Prince felt very deeply the disgrace of his father. He followed Yáhuar Huácac and, marching rapidly, overtook him. Covered with dust and sweat, with a lance in his hand, which he had obtained on the road, the Prince presented himself before the King, and, with a sad countenance, said:

"O Inca! How is it possible that you should desert your city and court and turn your back on the enemy before they are in sight? I like it not and I shall return to face the enemy before they can enter Cuzco. Those that will follow me, let them do so and I will show them how to choose between a disgraced life and an honored death."

Having said this with every sign of grief and sorrow, the Prince turned back along the road to Cuzco. The Incas of the blood royal, in number more than four thousand men, went with the Prince, leaving Yáhuar Huácac alone. On the road they met many fugitives flying from the city. They called to them to turn back, as the Prince was returning to defend the city. The Prince displayed so much resolution and bravery that he imparted new courage to all his followers. In this way he returned to Cuzco and ordered the people to take up a position between the rebels and the city.

News reached the Prince that the rebels had crossed the river Apurímac and were within nine or ten leagues of Cuzco. Two days after this bad news arrived, good news came that nearly twenty thousand men were coming to the Prince's aid from about sixty miles away.

The Prince stood by until the first reinforcements reached him, numbering twelve thousand fighting men. Five thousand additional warriors were only two days' journey away. The Prince sent orders to the second group of reinforcements to conceal themselves in certain hills and ravines in the vicinity. Once the rebels offered battle, the hidden troops were to attack them on one side so as to defeat them with greater ease.

Two days later the vanguard of the enemy was sighted. Prince Viracocha sent messages to the rebels offering peace and friendship, and pardon for the past. But the Chancas, having heard that Yáhuar Huácac had fled, knew the messages came from Prince Viracocha, and they sent away the messengers without hearing them.

The two armies were on watch all night. At daybreak the squadrons marched

against each other with loud cries and shouts, and the sound of trumpets and shells. The Prince advanced in front of his army, and was the first to hurl a missile against the enemy. At noon the five thousand Indians who had been ordered to conceal themselves suddenly appeared and attacked the rebels furiously on their right flank. The Chancas fell back, but recovering, fought desperately. The armies fought more than two long hours without apparent advantage to either side, but then the Chancas began to waver, for every hour fresh men from the neighboring villages joined the army of the Incas. These new troops entered the battle with loud shouts and ear-splitting yells which made a noise quite out of proportion to their numbers.

The Incas, accustomed to embellishing their deeds with fables, shouted aloud that the reinforcements were the stones and thickets of the plain which had been turned into fighting men by the god Viracocha. The Chancas, being a credulous people, began to despair. The Incas, seeing that the rebels were giving ground, charged with renewed fury, finally routing the enemy.

After this great victory, the Prince dispatched a messenger to the temple of the Sun to offer up thanks. He sent another messenger to his father Yáhuar Huácac, giving him an account of all that had happened, and requesting that the Inca stay where he was until the Prince returned.

The Prince then set out in pursuit of the enemy with six thousand soldiers. In a very short time he toured all the provinces that had rebelled. He marched back to Cuzco and re-entered the city on foot, to show that he was more a soldier than a king. The Prince was received with great rejoicing. Old Inca nobles came out to welcome him. His mother, his sisters, aunts, and first and second cousins welcomed him with festive and joyous songs. Some embraced him, others wiped the sweat from his face, others brushed the dust off his clothes, and others strewed flowers and scented herbs before him.

However, the Inca Yáhuar Huácac did not receive his son with great rejoicing and satisfaction, but with a grave and melancholy countenance, as if there were more cause for sorrow than for joy. Few words passed between father and son in public, but it is thought that they talked privately about who should reign.

After the conversation, the Prince decided that his father, who had abandoned Cuzco, should not return to the city, and the court agreed.

The Prince put aside his yellow fringe and adopted the red one of the ruling

The Inca Viracocha

Inca. But he never insisted that his father should stop wearing the red fringe.

The Inca Viracocha is said to have had hair on his face, while the Indians are usually beardless, and he wore his clothes down to his feet, which differs from the usual custom of the Indians, whose clothes come down to their knees.

After passing some years attending to the good government of his people, Viracocha decided to conquer those kingdoms which his father had not subdued. He gathered a new army together and appointed one of his brothers captain-general. Viracocha's military strength was such that no tribe was powerful enough to offer resistance, and he annexed great provinces with ease.

The Inca's dominions were now very extensive, for they reached eastward to the foot of the great snowy range of mountains, westward to the sea, and south to the most distant province of Charcas six hundred miles from Cuzco. But as the passion for dominion is insatiable, there arose in the mind of Viracocha a desire to extend his sway to the north.

After consulting his Council, he marched north with an army to a large province inhabited by a warlike people. The inhabitants surrendered as soon as the messengers of the Inca arrived. Thence Viracocha passed on to another province, and to others, all of which submitted cheerfully.

After visiting these new additions to his empire, Viracocha resolved to remain at his court in Cuzco and employed his time in governing his kingdom.

To the Inca Viracocha a prophecy is attributed which foretold that after a certain number of Incas had reigned, there would come to the land a people never seen before who would destroy the religion and empire of the natives. The Inca ordered that the prophecy should be revealed to the royal princes, but he did not permit it to be divulged to the common people, for it was not wise to admit that the Incas would fall from their high estate.

Later, when the Spaniards came to conquer Peru, the Indians gave them the name Viracocha, because they thought their arrival was a fulfillment of this prophecy, and because, like Viracocha, the Spaniards wore beards and were clothed from head to foot.

Viracocha ordered in his will that his eldest son and heir should be called Pachacútec, which means "he who overturns" or "he who changes the world." The Inca Viracocha died at the height of his power and majesty. It is commonly thought that his reign lasted more than fifty years.

PART II

From Garcilaso de la Vega

After solemnly observing the funeral rites of his father, Pachacútec Inca assembled an army to conquer more territory. He gave command of the troops to his brother Cápac Yupanqui, a gallant prince.

The Prince's forces marched to the province of Sausa, a most beautiful country inhabited by a tribe of Indians called Huancas.

The Huancas were a warlike people who burned prisoners taken in war, and made drums of their skins.

These Indians worshiped the figure of a dog. They considered the flesh of a dog to be most savory. To this day, when anyone refers to a Huanca, he generally adds "dog-eater."

Cápac Yupanqui conquered this powerful tribe and returned to Cuzco where his brother Pachacútec received him with festivities which lasted a moon.

Three years later Inca Pachacútec again put Cápac Yupanqui in command of an army. He sent with him the sixteen-year-old Prince Yupanqui, who was heir to the empire, so that the Prince could acquire experience in the art of war. First the army of the Inca entered the province called Pincu, where the inhabitants surrendered. But the other neighboring districts, instead of following the example of Pincu, rose in arms. General Cápac Yupanqui blockaded the people of these districts, and finally conquered them by cutting off their food supply.

Next the general accepted the surrender of a nation called Huamanchucu, which was ruled by a great chief of the same name.

The Incas then invaded Cajamarca, a large and fertile province. For four months the people of Cajamarca fought the Incas, but at last they too submitted.

These matters being settled, Cápac Yupanqui marched back to Cuzco. The Inca Pachacútec came out to receive his brother and his son the Prince with pride. He ordered that they should enter the city carried in litters on the shoulders of Indians from the areas they had just conquered.

Everyone who lived in Cuzco and many from outside the city marched in the procession. They played various songs composed in their own languages on their native instruments: drums, trumpets, horns, and shells. Behind the Indians marched the soldiers with their weapons in their hands. After the soldiers came the Incas of the blood royal carrying their arms. In the midst of the procession

The Inca Pachacútec

rode General Cápac Yupanqui with Prince Yupanqui on his right hand; and next to them rode the Inca Pachacútec in his litter of gold.

After three or four years without waging any war, the Incas turned their attention to the coast valleys. They marched to the province of Nanasca, and from there they sent messages to the inhabitants of the valley of Ica and the valley of Pisco demanding their submission. The natives of both valleys answered that they were willing to receive the Inca Pachacútec as their king.

The coast valleys are fertile, and in the period after the conquest there, the Incas built a splendid aqueduct to bring water down from high up in the mountains. In order to do this they changed the course of a river with great skill, making it run westward instead of eastward. With the help of this aqueduct they more than doubled the area of land under cultivation and thenceforward the Indians of the valleys lived in great abundance and prosperity.

After they had acquired the valleys of Ica and Pisco, the Incas sent word to the great and powerful people of a valley called Chincha, demanding that they bow down to the Inca Pachacútec, child of the Sun. The people of Chincha were defiant. They replied that the sun did them no good at all but rather annoyed them by its excessive heat, while those in the Sierra, where the country is cold, might well worship it, as they needed its heat. A war was carried on with great fury, and many were killed on both sides. The general Cápac Yupanqui finally declared that unless the Chinchas submitted within eight days he would put them all to death and people their valley with a new race of men. Alarmed by this threat, the Chinchas yielded. The Inca Pachacútec rejoiced to see an end to this troublesome war. He afterward adorned this beautiful valley with a grand temple to the Sun.

The Incas next proceeded to the valleys of Rímac, Pachacámac, Cháncay, and Huaman. All these valleys were held by a powerful lord named Cuismancu.

The valley of Rímac was named for an idol there, in the shape of a man, which spoke and gave answers to questions. Rímac was later corrupted by the Spaniards into the name Lima.

General Cápac Yupanqui demanded that King Cuismancu submit to the Inca Pachacútec, observing his laws and customs and worshiping the Sun as his principal god, or prepare for war. The great lord Cuismancu, who was already prepared for war, declared that his people had no wish to put away their gods, for

among them was Pachacámac, the creator and preserver of the universe, as well as the oracle Rímac.

The Incas also worshiped Pachacámac and were delighted to find that King Cuismancu and his people held him in equal veneration.

General Cápac Yupanqui decided to hold off fighting until he had spoken to Cuismancu at greater length on the subject of their gods. The general offered to accept Rímac as a sacred oracle for the Incas, and he proposed, by way of an exchange, that Cuismancu and his subjects should agree to worship the Sun. The general also proposed, to preserve peace and friendship, that King Cuismancu and his people should acknowledge the Inca Pachacútec as a child of the Sun.

King Cuismancu and his followers considered the matter for many days and finally agreed to these terms.

For six years after this the Inca Pachacútec desisted from the conquest of new provinces.

At the end of this period, he gathered troops together in preparation for a new campaign under the leadership of the young Prince Inca Yupanqui. The Prince consulted the oracle Rímac as to the success of the campaign. He was told that it would succeed.

The Prince then advanced to a valley called Huancu and dispatched the customary demands to surrender to a great lord named Chimu, chief of all the valleys beyond. The great and powerful Chimu replied that he was prepared to die with his weapons in his hands in the defense of his homeland. A fierce and cruel war ensued, but finally the lord Chimu submitted. The Prince then visited the surrounding valleys and ordered them adorned with grand edifices and enriched with irrigation channels. He also commanded that a fortress be erected in memory of his victory.

The Inca Pachacútec, now being old, devoted himself to the enactment of new laws for the common good. He founded towns, built more temples to the Sun, and enriched their walls with sheets of gold. He repaired many storehouses on the royal roads and built houses where the Incas might lodge when traveling. He also reformed the army, enlarged the great city of Cuzco, and constructed a palace for himself near the schools founded by his great-grandfather Inca Roca. He reigned more than fifty years. At the end of this time, he died.

The good Inca Yupanqui took possession of the empire and visited his dominions. After this tour, he decided to undertake a campaign east of Cuzco in the direction of the great chain of snowy mountains. He resolved to cross the mountains by descending a river that flows to the east. He ordered a great quantity of timber cut to build enough canoes to hold ten thousand warriors, along with their supplies. The Incas then started downstream.

After a long journey and many bitter skirmishes with hostile Indians along the banks of the river, they reached the province of Musu, six hundred miles from Cuzco. The Musus were so astonished to see the Incas and so interested in hearing about their empire that they wished to be friends. However, they refused to be vassals, for they wanted to be as free as their fathers had been before them. The Incas honored the Musus' wishes, and the friendship between the two tribes lasted until the arrival of the Spaniards.

Inca Yupanqui next resolved to conquer the kingdom of Chile. After reducing the valley of Chile to submission, the Incas marched 150 miles to the south, subduing the tribes as far as the river Maule. But when they crossed this river they were met by an alliance of tribes who were determined to die rather than lose their ancient liberty. The armies attacked each other with great fury and bravery. They fought for three days, and many of the warriors were killed or wounded.

At the end of that time, both sides retired. The Incas resolved to withdraw to the territory they had already conquered and to fix the river Maule as the boundary of their empire.

The King Inca Yupanqui made an end of the conquest of new territory, seeing that his empire was now more than a thousand leagues in length, and resolved to pass the rest of his life enobling his kingdom. He especially occupied himself in the construction of the fortress of Cuzco, which his father had left unfinished.

At last he fell sick, and, feeling his end approaching, he sent for his heir Túpac Inca Yupanqui. Thus he died full of good and great deeds.

Túpac Inca Yupanqui, whose name means "he who shines," assumed the crimson fringe on the death of his father.

The great Inca Túpac Yupanqui conquered many rugged provinces and villages such as Chachapoya, Papamarca ("the village of potatoes"), and Huan-

The Inca Túpac Yupanqui

capampa. Tired with the fatigue of these campaigns, he spent several years beautifying his dominions. He also continued the construction of the fortress at Cuzco.

The Inca then undertook the conquest of provinces farther north. He came to the one called Huánucu and easily reduced it to submission.

We have related the conquest of Huánucu briefly, as we shall do that of the other provinces, for I now desire to reach the end of the conquests of the Inca kings and to treat of the war between Huáscar and Atahuallpa, grandsons of Túpac Yupanqui.

Túpac Yupanqui commenced new expeditions and gained many provinces up to the great and famous kingdom of Quito.

After passing some years of peace, the Inca resolved to conquer Quito, which was 210 miles long and ninety miles broad. He assembled an army of forty thousand men and sent the usual demand to the King of Quito, who had the same name as his country. Confident of his strength, Quito proudly replied that he was master and that he would acknowledge no other. A war broke out which lasted for many years, with skirmishes and indecisive battles in which great numbers were killed and wounded on both sides. Seeing that the conquest would take a long time, Túpac Yupanqui sent for reinforcements of twelve thousand men under the command of his son and heir, Huaina Cápac. The name of this prince means "the rich youth."

Huaina Cápac, who was then about twenty years of age, continued the war and began to gain territory little by little.

Túpac Yupanqui, seeing the excellent way in which the Prince was conducting the war, returned to Cuzco, leaving Huaina Cápac with absolute military power. The Prince, assisted by his captains, conquered Quito in three years, then marched back to Cuzco to report to his father.

At this time Huaina Cápac contracted his second marriage with his second sister, as he had had no children by his first wife, his eldest sister, and according to Inca law it was necessary that the heir to the throne be in the direct line of descent on both the father's and the mother's sides.

After some years, the Inca Túpac Yupanqui fell ill. He summoned Prince Huaina Cápac and the rest of his numerous sons. He made a special request to the Prince to punish the treason committed by the Indians around Puerto

Viejo, in having killed those Inca captains and ministers who had been sent into their land to instruct them in civilization.

He then bade his people farewell. The Indians embalmed his body, and I saw it in the year 1559, when it looked as though it was alive.

The powerful Huaina Cápac set out to inspect his dominions. Wherever he went, the Curacas and Indians came forth to cover the roads with flowers and to build triumphal arches.

Soon after this, Huaina Cápac's second wife bore him a son and heir, Huascar Inca. Huaina Cápac rejoiced greatly. He planned a grand festival to celebrate the day when his son would be weaned.

It seemed to the Inca that it would increase the majesty of the celebration if the Indian dancers performed holding onto a chain instead of taking hands. He therefore designed for the festival a chain of gold which later became famous throughout the world. Besides the common report, I heard a special account of the golden chain from the old Inca, my uncle. I asked him about the length of the chain and he told me that it was twice the width and length of the great square at Cuzco. The length of this square was about two hundred ordinary paces of two feet each; and its width was about 150 paces, including the space occupied by the houses built by the Spaniards in 1556, when my father Garcilaso de la Vega was Corregidor of that great city. According to this measurement, the golden chain must have been about seven hundred feet long. When I asked my uncle about its thickness, he put out his thumb and said that each length was of that thickness.

The Indians concealed this rich and noble piece of work, along with many other treasures, as soon as the Spaniards entered the country. Though searched for diligently, the chain has never been found.

A year after the festival, Huaina Cápac traveled to the kingdom of Quito. There he married his third wife, the eldest daughter of the former king of the province, and had by her a son Atahuallpa, whom we shall meet with later in this history.

From Quito Huaina Cápac proceeded to the valley of Chimu. His troops conquered the natives there along with those in neighboring valleys.

Next he marched into the provinces around Puerto Viejo where the officers, ministers, and masters whom his father had sent had been killed. As punishment

for their crimes the Inca put to death one-tenth of the traitors. Then he set out and visited half his empire, the extreme south of Peru, intending next to visit the other half, which is more to the east. On his way eastward, Huaina Cápac received news that the great province of the Chachapoyas had rebelled. The Indians there had killed the governors and captains and many of the soldiers of the Incas. Huaina Cápac ordered his troops to march to Chachapoya, where he intended to inflict severe chastisement. The rebels began to fear punishment, but remembered that a weakness of Huaina Cápac's was that he could never refuse a petition made by a woman, whatever her age, rank, or condition. So they sent to him a Chachapoya matron, accompanied by many other women of all ages, without any man whatsoever. The women all threw themselves at his feet, and the matron said: "O sole lord, do not proceed in your anger to destroy a province which your father conquered and added to his empire. Consider that however great the crime of these wretched people, so much more glorious will be your mercy."

The Inca approached the matron. Raising her from the ground, he said: "I well see that you are a mother, seeing that you watch over my honor from afar and advise me how to honor the memory of the majesty of my father. I am deeply grateful to you, for there is no doubt that tomorrow I would regret having indulged my anger today. You have been like a good mother to us all. Return to your people, and pardon them in my name." Having said this, he returned to his army.

Huaina Cápac was saddened that these insurrections occurred during his reign, for nothing of the kind had ever happened, except the revolt of the Chancas in the days of the Inca Viracocha. As a matter of fact, these rebellions were warnings of a greater insurrection, which would lead to the fall of the empire, and the total destruction of the royal family.

Huaina Cápac, as has already been mentioned, had a son named Atahuallpa, by the daughter of the King of Quito. Atahuallpa grew up with good understanding. He was quick-witted, sagacious, cunning, and cautious; and in war brave and enterprising. He was handsome and had a noble bearing.

His father loved Atahuallpa dearly and would have liked to make him heir to the whole empire. But he could not deprive his eldest son and legitimate heir, Huáscar Inca, of his rights. However, contrary to the laws of his ances-

The Inca Huaina Cápac

tors, he resolved to take away from Huáscar the kingdom of Quito, coloring his action with some appearance of justice. He summoned Prince Huáscar, who was then in Cuzco, to come to Quito. On the Prince's arrival, Huaina Cápac called together a great assembly of his sons, and his captains and Curacas. In their presence he addressed his legitimate son, Huáscar: "As I love your brother Atahuallpa, and as it would grieve me to see him poor, I request that you will see fit to leave him the inheritance of the kingdom of Quito, which belonged to his maternal ancestors. Thus he will be able to live in a royal state, as his virtues merit; and I shall leave this world contented, when I go to rest with our father the Sun."

The Prince Huáscar Inca answered, very promptly, that he extremely rejoiced to obey the Inca his father in this or in anything else he might see fit to order.

Huaina Cápac was well satisfied with this answer, and he prepared to leave Atahuallpa in possession of the kingdom of Quito.

Huaina Cápac was occupied with these affairs, and was in the royal palaces of Tumipampa, the most superb in Peru, when news arrived that strange people, such as had never been seen in the land, were sailing in a ship along the coast of the Inca Empire. This news made Huaina Cápac very anxious to ascertain what people these might be and whence they came. (The ship was that of Balboa, first discoverer of the South Sea, and it was the Spaniards on that ship who gave the name of Peru to the empire in the year 1515.)

Huaina Cápac passed the remaining eight years of his life quietly governing his empire. He had no desire to make new conquests, but he was on the lookout for whatever might come from the sea, for he felt great anxiety, remembering the ancient prophetic warning that, after a certain number of Inca kings had reigned, a strange people would arrive and deprive the Incas of their kingdom.

It must also be known that an evil omen had occurred in Cuzco three years before the news of the strange ship. A royal eagle was pursued by five or six kestrels and other little hawks. They attacked the eagle alternately and wounded him by their blows. The eagle, unable to defend himself, fell into the middle of the great square of the city.

The Indians fed him and treated him kindly, but nothing availed, and in a

few days he died, without having been able to raise himself from the ground.

There were also great earthquakes and tremors at this time. Furthermore, the Indians of the coast reported that the sea often extended beyond its usual bounds; and they saw awful comets in the air. In the midst of these forebodings, the coast Indians reported that on a very clear night the moon had three great circles around it. The first was the color of blood. The second was black, turning to green. The third looked like smoke.

On one of the last days of his life, Huaina Cápac, who was visiting the kingdom of Quito, entered a lake to bathe. He came out with a trembling chill on him. Feeling ill, he summoned his children and relations, and the governors and captains of neighboring provinces, and thus addressed them:

"I go to rest in Heaven with our father the Sun, who long long ago revealed to me that I should be summoned either from a river or a lake. I commend you to my son Atahuallpa, whom I so dearly love and who will remain as Inca in my place in this kingdom of Quito. I especially desire the captains of my army to serve him with fidelity and love; and they are to obey him in all things and do as he commands them."

He sent for the other Curacas and captains who were not of the blood royal and said:

"Many years ago it was revealed by our father the Sun that after twelve of his kingly children had reigned, a strange people would arrive, such as had never before been seen in these parts, and that this people would conquer and subjugate our kingdoms and many others. I suspect that some of them have already appeared in the seas off our coast. They will be a brave people who will overcome us in everything. We also know that in me is completed the number of twelve Incas. I foretell to you that a few years after I have departed, this race will come, and will conquer our empire, and will be lords of it. I order you to obey and serve them, as men who have the advantage of you in all things, whose laws will be better than ours, and whose arms will be more powerful and invincible. Peace be with you; I go to rest with my father the Sun, who has called me."

Huaina Cápac died leaving more than two hundred sons and daughters.

After the death of Huaina Cápac, Huáscar Inca began to reflect that he had not done well in consenting to the demand of his father concerning the king-

dom of Quito, which had been given to his brother Atahuallpa. Huáscar sent a message to Atahuallpa, saying that by the ancient laws of the first Inca Manco Cápac, which were respected by all his descendants, the kingdom of Quito belonged to the Inca crown in Cuzco. He had, he said, complied with the demand of his father, but it had been a forced obedience, and not a submission to a just decree. His father ought not have made such a demand, nor was he bound to obey it. But, as he had already consented, he would gladly abide by the decree on two conditions. One was that Atahuallpa should not extend the boundaries of Quito by a single hair's breadth. The other was that Atahuallpa should acknowledge himself to be a vassal of Huáscar Inca.

After considering the matter, Atahuallpa answered with much sagacity, caution, and astuteness. He said that, in his heart, he had always acknowledged himself to be a vassal of Huáscar Inca, and that not only would he refrain from adding to his kingdom, but that, if Huáscar desired it, he would renounce the kingdom of Quito.

Huáscar Inca was well satisfied and answered that he was pleased to let his brother keep possession of Quito as his father had wished. He announced that to confirm the grant, Atahuallpa should come to Cuzco and do him homage faithfully and loyally.

Atahuallpa answered that he would come to express his obedience, and to make his submission more solemn, he asked for permission to bring people from all the provinces of Quito to celebrate the funeral rites of their father in Cuzco. Huáscar Inca granted all his brother's requests.

Atahuallpa ordered a proclamation made throughout his dominion that all able-bodied men should prepare to march to Cuzco to celebrate the funeral rites of the great Huaina Cápac and to take the oath of homage to the monarch Huáscar Inca. For both ceremonies they were ordered to bring festive dresses and ornaments.

But at the same time Atahuallpa gave orders to his captains that each one should select his bravest warriors and instruct them to secretly bring their arms so that they would be ready to do battle with and conquer the forces of Huáscar. The warriors were ordered to march in squadrons and to pretend to be servants and not soldiers. By this arrangement Atahuallpa sent forward more than thirty thousand soldiers (most of them chosen veterans whom his father,

the Inca Huaina Cápac, had left) with famous and experienced captains.

The men of Quito marched until they were within a hundred leagues of Cuzco. Some old Incas, governors of provinces through which they passed, began to feel some alarm on seeing so large a force. They sent secret warnings to Huáscar Inca, entreating him to be on guard. These warnings awoke Huáscar from his sleep of confidence. He sent messengers to gather all his troops together.

The troops of Atahuallpa were experienced soldiers, and went looking for Huáscar Inca, to attack him before he could be joined by all his forces. A desperate battle was fought on a great plain to the west of Cuzco. It lasted all day, and many were killed on both sides. The troops of Atahuallpa won the victory. They captured Huáscar Inca, for they knew that they would have achieved nothing if he had been permitted to escape.

Atahuallpa made a most cruel use of his victory. He pretended that it was his intention to restore Huáscar to the throne, and on this pretext he summoned all the Incas in the empire, as well as governors and ministers of peace, masters of the camp and war captains, to Cuzco. All the Incas of the blood royal obeyed the summons. When they were gathered together, Atahuallpa had them put to death in different ways, so that he might feel secure against any insurrection that they might otherwise have attempted.

The poor Inca Huáscar was not put to death, but was reserved as a hostage in the event that a rebellion might arise, since Atahuallpa knew that the Indians would obey any order from Huáscar.

A few Incas escaped from Atahuallpa. One of them was my mother, another was her brother, named Don Francisco Huallpa Túpac Inca Yupanqui.

All this and much more was told to me by the old Inca my uncle who was enraged at the thought of the destruction of all his relations; and of the evil that the cruelties of Atahuallpa had caused.

The Inca Huáscar

PART III

From Pedro Pizarro

In the city of Panama in the early 1500's there lived three wealthy Spanish conquerors; the Marquis Don Francisco Pizarro, Don Diego de Almagro, and Father Luque. These men were associated in several land grants. Don Francisco was the most important of the three. He had been a captain in the conquest of Panama.

News came to Panama of a province called Peru. It was said to be a very mountainous country inhabited by fierce Indians who used poisoned arrows.

Pizarro, Almagro, and Father Luque agreed to explore the province. Pizarro was named captain-general of the expedition, and Almagro was appointed second leader. They embarked with and sailed down the coast of South America until they reached the northernmost part of Peru. Because of hostile Indians on the shore, they could not land, so they continued on.

Two years were spent in this journey, during which more than three hundred men died of hunger and disease. At the end of this time the Spaniards reached a port on the island of Gallo, so shattered and greatly enfeebled that they were unable to proceed farther. It was agreed that Pizarro would remain on the island with the few men who were left, and that Almagro would return to Panama to gather more troops and supplies.

Almagro made the return journey and dispatched the additional men to Pizarro on a ship commanded by Bartolomé Pérez.

When Pérez arrived at Gallo, he was met with joy by the Spaniards, for they were on the point of perishing with hunger, and had been attacked repeatedly by the Indians of the island.

Reinforced and refreshed, Pizarro and his men boarded their ships and continued on their journey.

They soon discovered good land at a place they called Puerto Viejo. The Indians of the vicinity worshiped the Sun as their most important god, and also worshiped stones and wooden idols.

From Puerto Viejo the Spaniards sailed to the port of Túmbez, where the natives were very warlike. For arms they had long arrows, spears, and clubs.

The expedition proceeded south, and a little farther down the coast they encountered some native canoes. They captured the canoes, along with three or

four Indian boys, and several belts made of mother-of-pearl, gold, and silver.

After giving thanks to God for having vouchsafed them so many mercies, and for showing them a land so rich and well peopled, Pizarro sailed back toward Panama. From there he planned to proceed to Spain in order to give His Majesty the King an account of all he had discovered.

Back in Panama, Pizarro, Almagro, and Father Luque agreed that Pizarro should seek from the King a joint governorship of the province of Peru for himself and Almagro, and a bishopric for Father Luque.

Pizarro set out for Spain carrying with him the Indian boys and all the gold, silver, and mother-of-pearl which he had brought from Peru.

Up to this point, I, Pedro Pizarro, tell what was told to me. Henceforth I shall tell what I have seen with my own eyes.

Francisco Pizarro was by the grace of our Lord borne safely to Spain where he had an audience with His Majesty the Emperor, who is now in glory. When Pizarro had given the Emperor an account of what had been discovered, His Majesty sent him to the Council of the Indies. Pizarro made the requests that he had agreed upon with Almagro and Father Luque. But the Council informed him that it was not a good idea for the governorship of Peru to be given to two companions, because this had been done once before in connection with another province, and one governor had killed the other. Pizarro was therefore advised to ask for the governorship for himself alone. He did this, and his request was granted.

Pizarro then went to the port of Seville where he engaged two ships and a smaller vessel to carry some of the King's troops to Panama and on to Peru.

While he was waiting for a favorable time to sail, Don Francisco was warned that some Spanish officials were coming to review the troops and that he could not leave Seville if he had not collected three hundred men by the time the officials arrived. Realizing that he would not have the required number in time, Pizarro embarked with a few troops on the small vessel and sailed to the island of Gomera.

When the officials came to hold the review they found that Pizarro had gone. The remaining troops convinced the officials that Pizarro had taken enough men with him to make up the required three hundred.

In a few days the other ships sailed out under the command of Hernando Pizarro, Don Francisco's brother. I, Pedro Pizarro, sailed with him.

Our Lord being pleased to vouchsafe us good weather, we arrived at Gomera where we found Don Francisco. From Gomera we all sailed back across the Atlantic to Panama.

In Panama our men heard rumors that Peru was a bad land with nothing to eat but serpents and lizards and dogs. This news filled our men with fear, causing many of them to flee from us.

Soon after we landed, Don Diego de Almagro came to meet with Don Francisco. When Almagro understood that His Majesty had given the governorship of Peru to Don Francisco alone, he was furious. He took himself off with all the money he had collected, and insisted that he would not aid Don Francisco in preparing the fleet for the return expedition to Peru.

Father Luque also withdrew because Pizarro had not brought him the bishopric agreed upon.

On account of these incidents, much hardship was experienced.

There were also some disagreements between Almagro and Hernando Pizarro. On one occasion Almagro went to visit Hernando and they discussed preparations for the return journey. Hernando told Almagro that he was much disturbed because he had not been able to supply horses for two of his officers. Almagro gave his word that he himself would give each of the officers a horse, but he did not keep his promise. For this reason Hernando used evil language to Almagro, calling him a roistering scoundrel and other offensive things.

It soon befell that Hernando Ponce de León and Hernando de Soto came to Panama with two ships laden with slaves. Don Francisco was eager to acquire the ships for his expedition. He made an agreement with the two men whereby they gave him the ships. In return the Marquis placed Soto in command of both vessels, and agreed to make Soto captain and lieutenant governor of the chief town which should be found in Peru. And Hernán Ponce was guaranteed one of the best land grants in that kingdom.

Don Diego de Almagro now saw that the journey to Peru could be accomplished without his support. He therefore made friends again with Don Francisco Pizarro and Hernando Pizarro, although he did this with reservations and evil designs.

All that I have described having been arranged, Don Francisco embarked with his troops, in all some two hundred men.

The Spaniards arrived at a Peruvian village called Coaqui, where they at-

tacked the natives without warning and captured a vast quantity of gold and silver. They collected all the valuables in one place. They were forbidden on pain of death to hide any away for themselves, for the Marquis planned to distribute the treasure, giving to each man a quantity in conformity with his merits and services.

Many fine objects of gold and silver were found: many pieces made of gold after the fashion of imperial crowns, and many other pieces the value of which amounted to more than two hundred thousand castellanos. Don Francisco sent one of the ships which he had obtained from Hernán Ponce de León back to Panama with some of these objects, to display them so that other troops might be encouraged to come to Peru.

While the Spaniards were in Coaqui, about thirty more men arrived from Panama in a small vessel. This gave great joy to the Marquis and his troops.

As the Spaniards prepared to begin their journey overland, they received news of an island called Puna. They boarded their ships and sailed to the island. The chief of Puna, who was named Tumpalla, seemed to be friendly, and gave the Spaniards a peaceful reception. But at the end of some days Tumpalla devised a plot to slay them.

Tumpalla came to the headquarters of the Marquis while his Indian troops made a great noise which he told the Marquis was the sound of dancing. Actually they were making all the noise because they were fully armed. There was a surprise attack in which some of the Spaniards were wounded, among them Hernando Pizarro, who received a leg injury. The Marquis's troops, however, won the day and held Tumpalla and some of his chief men prisoners for several days.

When the Indians of the nearby port of Túmbez heard that Tumpalla was a prisoner, they came to Puna feigning peaceful intentions toward the Spaniards.

Just at this time Hernando de Soto returned from Panama with two ships full of fresh troops. His arrival greatly encouraged the Marquis as his men had been lacking in food, and the greater part of his troops had been sick. To add to the Spaniards' unhappiness, they had not found any gold or silver on Puna.

After several days, the Marquis decided he would proceed to Túmbez. He ordered most of his soldiers and all of his horses aboard the Spanish ships. The rest of the men embarked with the Túmbez Indians in some balsa canoes.

It soon became clear that the Indians' purpose was treachery. They put their

passengers ashore on some small islands for the night. When the Spaniards fell asleep, the Indians slipped away in the canoes. Later they returned with more Indians and killed the sleeping men.

The same thing would have happened to Francisco Martín, a brother of the Marquis, and to Alonso de Mesa, and to me, had it not been for the fact that Alonso de Mesa was very sick and had not gotten out of his canoe. When Mesa saw our companions being killed by the Indians, he gave great shouts which awakened Francisco Martín and me. We immediately bound the chief and the other Indians and stayed on watch all night.

The next day we set out again and soon were within sight of Túmbez. When we came near the shore the Indians manning our canoes threw themselves into the water, dragging us with them into the rough surf. However, the waves cast us up on land. Seeing that we were safely on shore, the angry Indians pushed off, taking with them all our supplies and belongings.

When the Marquis and the rest of the men arrived at Túmbez, they discovered what had happened to most of the Spaniards in the canoes. There was great discontent in the ranks, and the soldiers cursed the Marquis for leading them to a land so remote and so desolate. For they had not yet an inkling of the greatness of Peru.

In the midst of this unsettled state of affairs, it befell that a friendly Indian came to Túmbez and told the Marquis that a civil war was raging in Cuzco. The Indian said that the Spaniards seemed to be powerful men of war who were destined to conquer everything. When the Indian was asked what Cuzco might be, he replied that it was a great town where the King of all the Indians of Peru lived. He said that the town was well populated, and that the inhabitants had many vessels of gold and silver, and objects inlaid with plates of gold. The Indian told the truth, and there was even more than he said. But the Spaniards were so downcast that they did not believe the Indian, saying it was a trick of the Marquis who had told him what to say in order to encourage them.

With matters still unsettled, the Marquis heard about a valley called Pohechos. He set forth for this place, taking Hernando de Soto and some troops with him. He left his brother Hernando Pizarro behind with the rest of the men, who were sick, in order that little by little they might follow him.

At Pohechos the Marquis received word that the Inca Atahuallpa was on his way from Quito to Cajamarca, waging war upon his brother Huáscar, the right-

ful ruler of the Indians of Peru. When he heard this, Don Francisco sent Hernando de Soto to Cajamarca with some cavalry to bring back news of the province and to learn more about Atahuallpa and his forces.

Hernando de Soto stayed away more time than he had been granted, which created a suspicion in the camp that all was not going well. During this period of anxiety Hernando Pizarro arrived with his men.

Meanwhile certain other Spaniards who were in the Chira valley, discovering that the Indians there wished to kill them, retired to a fortress and sent a messenger asking the Marquis for help. Soto had finally returned from Cajamarca bearing news of Atahuallpa, and the Marquis set out for the Chira valley with Soto and some cavalry. He left the remainder of the troops under the command of Hernando Pizarro.

While Hernando Pizarro was in command at Pohechos, Atahuallpa, wanting news of the invaders, sent a disguised Inca captain, called an *apu*, to see what manner of men the Spaniards were and to make the acquaintance of their leader.

The disguised *apu*, pretending that it was his purpose to beg forgiveness for some Indian chiefs who had ceased to serve Hernando, brought the Spanish leader a basket of guanos, a native fruit. When the *apu* arrived, Hernando arose in great wrath, and taking the Indian by his scarf, threw him on the ground and gave him many kicks. The *apu* hid his face so as not to be known, and stole away. Then he went to give news to Atahuallpa of what he had seen and what had befallen him.

At Cajamarca, the *apu* told Atahuallpa that the Spaniards were bearded robbers who had come out of the sea, and that the soldiers rode upon animals much larger than any in the Inca Empire.

Meanwhile the Marquis, having rescued the Spaniards in the Chira valley, founded a settlement called Tangarala. This was the first town founded in Peru by the Spanish. Later the settlement was relocated in the Piura valley, where it is now established.

The Marquis then sent word to his brother Juan Pizarro to ride to the Piura valley with fifty horsemen and establish himself there with a large watch consisting of many spies to watch the doings of Atahuallpa's forces.

Hernando Pizarro was ordered to march from Pohechos to Tangarala with the rest of the men.

Then Don Francisco set out with his troops for Cajamarca, letting it be

known among the natives of Peru that he was going to favor and assist Huáscar, the rightful King Inca, who had been defeated and imprisoned by the captains of Atahuallpa.

On his way, Don Francisco was met by the Indian who had been misused by Hernando Pizarro. The *apu* craftily presented the Marquis with two shirts decorated with silver and gold, saying that they were gifts from Atahuallpa. However, the Indian had actually come to count how many men there were in Don Francisco's force. In order to do this without arousing suspicion, he went from one Spaniard to another, testing each man's strength and asking each to draw his sword and show it to him.

Then the *apu* returned to his lord Atahuallpa and related that he had counted some one hundred and ninety Spaniards, about ninety of whom were cavalry. The *apu* said that all the Spaniards were very full of fear and would flee when they saw Atahuallpa's troops. With this news Atahuallpa took courage, and he decided the Spaniards were of small account. Had he held them in fear, he would have sent troops to the mountains, which are very difficult and rugged, with treacherous passes. If he had stationed even a third of his troops at the passes he could have killed all the Spaniards. But our Lord ordered matters differently because it was in His service that the Christians entered Peru.

The Marquis, traveling by forced marches, crossed over the mountains and arrived at Cajamarca. Atahuallpa was at some baths more than a league from the town. His camp was established here and, as we later learned, it was filled with more than forty thousand warriors.

On the day of his arrival, the Marquis sent Hernando de Soto with twenty cavalrymen to Atahuallpa to tell him that Pizarro had come on behalf of God and the King of Spain to preach and to make friends, and to say that Pizarro was coming to see Atahuallpa.

Soto found Atahuallpa with all his troops in readiness for war. Atahuallpa was seated in a small house. According to the custom of the Incas, a very fine thin mantle, held by two women, covered him so that no one should see him. Atahuallpa ordered the women to lower the mantle, in order to hear all that Soto had to say. An interpreter made Soto's message clear to him.

Atahuallpa told Soto to return to the Marquis and announce to him and all the other Christians that on the following day, he, Atahuallpa, would come to the town of Cajamarca with his troops. He told Soto to tell the Marquis that he

expected to be repaid for all the gold and silver that had been taken from his kingdom by the Spaniards, as well as for all the food they had eaten, and that they were to make ready for his coming. Hearing this, Soto was dismayed.

Then Atahuallpa commanded his Indians to attack Soto's cavalry. But the Indians rose and fled, frightened by the charging horses. Atahuallpa commanded that the Indians who had run away should be put to death, so that no others would flee when the time came for the battle with the Marquis's troops.

Soto returned to the Marquis and with a good deal of fear gave an account of all that had befallen. The Spaniards spent the entire night on guard.

The same night, Atahuallpa dispatched twenty thousand soldiers to cut off the rear guard of the Spaniards, for he believed that they would take flight when they saw the size of his forces.

At dawn the Marquis arranged his troops, dividing his cavalry into two parts. He gave command of one group to Hernando Pizarro and command of the other group to Hernando de Soto. In like manner he divided the infantry, he himself taking one part and giving the other to his brother Juan Pizarro.

At the same time he ordered Pedro de Candía with two or three infantry-men to go to a fort in the plaza of Cajamarca and station themselves there with a small cannon. It was arranged that when Atahuallpa entered the plaza the infantrymen would make a signal, after which the firing would begin and the trumpets would sound. At the signal of the trumpets the cavalry would charge out of the large *galpón* (a passageway) leading to the plaza. The *galpón* had many wide doors, so that the cavalry could easily dash out mounted.

At the same time, Don Francisco and his brother Juan would wait in another part of the same *galpón* so that they could come out after the cavalry. All the Spaniards decked their horses' trappings with bells so that the sounds would fill the Indians with fear.

When the Spaniards were all arranged according to this plan, the news was carried to Atahuallpa by his spies that all the Spaniards were full of fear, hiding behind doors in a *galpón*, and that none of them dared to appear in the plaza. (And indeed the Indian spies told the truth, for I have heard that many of the Spaniards made water without knowing it, out of sheer terror.)

Later in the day, after having dined, Atahuallpa drew up his men and began to march toward Cajamarca. His squadrons were formed in such wise they covered the fields. Atahuallpa himself was carried in a litter. Before him went

two thousand Indians who swept the road on which he was traveling. Behind the sweepers came the warriors, marching on both sides of the road. Also, there marched with Atahuallpa many Indians singing and dancing.

The Indian troops arrived at the entrance of the plaza, and began to enter it to the accompaniment of great songs. Soon they occupied every part of the plaza. The Marquis, seeing that Atahuallpa had now drawn near to the plaza, sent the priest Fray Vicente de Valverde, who later became first bishop of Cuzco, Hernando de Aldama, a brave soldier, and Don Martinillo, an interpreter, to speak to Atahuallpa and require of him in the name of God and the King of Spain that he subject himself to the law of our Lord Jesus Christ and to the service of His Majesty, and to say that the Marquis would regard him as a brother and would not allow any injury to be done to him, nor any damage to be done to the land.

The priest came up to Atahuallpa's litter and began preaching unto the Indian matters pertaining to our holy faith. Our interpreter translated the priest's words into Atahuallpa's language. The priest carried a prayer book. Atahuallpa asked to see it, but when he had it in his hands he did not know how to open it and threw it upon the ground. The priest called upon Aldama to draw his sword, and Aldama brandished it, but did not wish to plunge it into the Inca. When this occurred, Atahuallpa dismissed them with rough insults, saying he was going to have all the Spaniards put to death. Hearing this, the priest returned to Pizarro and related all that had happened.

Atahuallpa entered the plaza in all his pomp, accompanied by an Inca of the blood royal in a second litter. When he saw that no Spaniard made his appearance, he asked his captains where the Christians were. They said to him, "Lord, they are in hiding for fear."

The Marquis, seeing the two litters, did not know which was that of Atahuallpa, so he ordered his brother Juan to attack one while he attacked the other. He then signaled Candía, who began to fire the cannon and sound the trumpets. The cavalry came out of the *galpón* in troop formation, followed by the Marquis with his foot soldiers. It all happened in such wise that, with the noise of the firing, and the blowing of the trumpets and the sound of the horses' bells, the Indians were thrown into confusion and were cut to pieces.

The Indians' fear and their anxiety to flee were so great that, not being able to pass through the gateway of the plaza, they broke through a portion of the

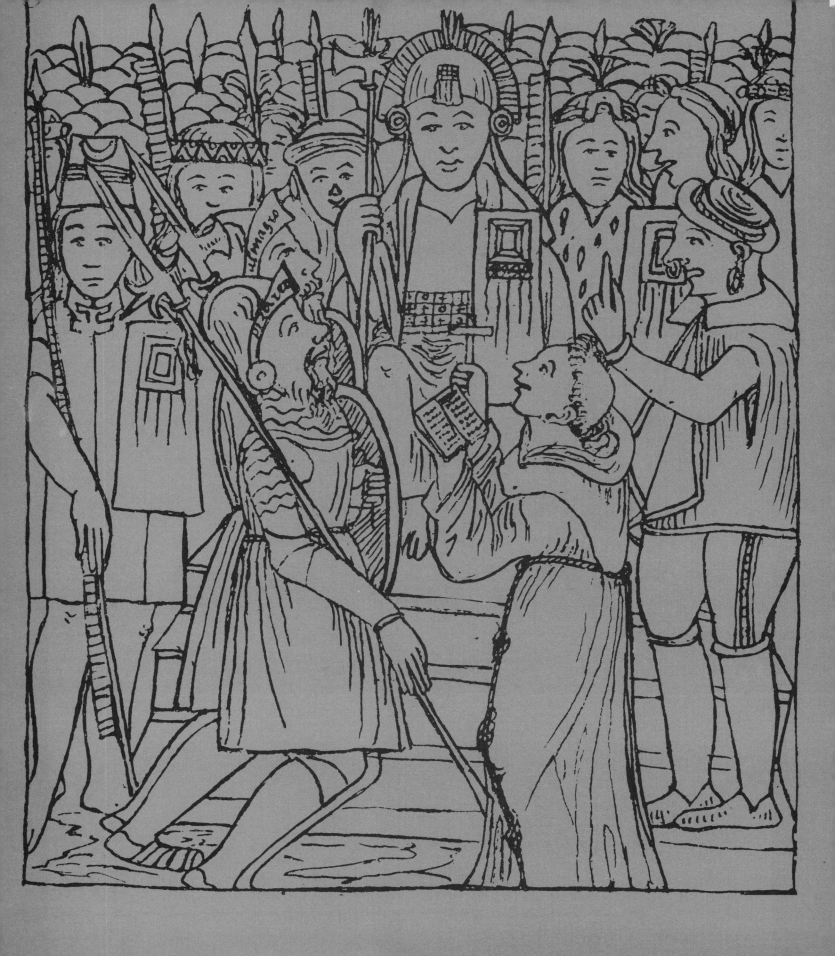

plaza wall. The Spanish cavalry pursued them and wrought great havoc among them.

Don Francisco and his brother then charged with their troops. The Marquis attacked the litter of Atahuallpa and Juan attacked the second litter, whose occupant was killed immediately. The same fate would have befallen Atahuallpa, had not the Marquis been there. A Spanish soldier was about to kill Atahuallpa with a knife, but Don Francisco prevented it. In doing so, he received a wound in the hand from the Spaniard.

The Marquis gave loud cries, saying: "Let no one wound the Indian on pain of death!" Hearing these words, seven or eight Spanish soldiers came rushing upon the litter from one side and, with great efforts, turned it over. Thus was Atahuallpa made a prisoner. The Marquis carried Atahuallpa off and set a guard over him to watch him day and night.

Then, night having fallen, all the Spaniards gathered together and gave many thanks to our Lord for the mercies vouchsafed to them. They were well content with having made Atahuallpa a prisoner, because had they not taken him so, Peru would not have been won as easily as it was won.

Atahuallpa feared that the Spaniards would kill him, because he understood that the Marquis was supporting his brother Huáscar, who was now held prisoner by Atahuallpa's captains. On the morrow Atahuallpa asked to speak to the Marquis. When the interpreter came, Atahuallpa bade him say to the Marquis that it would not be well to kill him and that he would give the Marquis much gold and silver. Hearing this the Marquis ordered Atahuallpa brought before him. Atahuallpa repeated what he had said to the interpreter.

The Marquis asked Atahuallpa how much gold and silver he would give. Atahuallpa said that as his ransom he would fill with gold the room where the Marquis was, and that he would twice fill with silver the big *galpón* where the Spaniards had assembled. In truth a great treasure!

The Marquis called a notary to put down in writing what the Indian promised. At the same time he asked Atahuallpa: "On whose behalf have you ordered this treasure?"

Atahuallpa replied: "On behalf of all the Spaniards who are in Cajamarca."

The Spaniards who were then in Caxamalca numbered about two hundred. This declaration by Atahuallpa, made before a notary, turned out to be the cause of his death, as will be related further on. When his offer was drawn up, Ata-

huallpa dispatched his captains to bring the treasure of gold and silver.

After this command was given by Atahuallpa, the Marquis made inquiries of him concerning the whereabouts of his brother, Huáscar. Atahuallpa replied that his captains held Huáscar prisoner. The Marquis ordered Atahuallpa to have Huáscar brought to Cajamarca and he ordered that Huáscar should not be killed, for if he were, Atahuallpa himself would be killed.

Meanwhile, some of the Indians who had escaped from the Spaniards fled to Atahuallpa's captains who were holding Huáscar and spread the rumor that Atahuallpa had been killed by the Christians, and many soldiers with him. Atahuallpa's captains did not know what to do, for they had greatly mistreated Huáscar in prison, and they did not dare to let him go free.

While things were in this state, Atahuallpa's messengers arrived and told the captains that he was alive. They also said that Atahuallpa had ordered the captains to gather together all the treasure in the land and send it to Cajamarca.

When Huáscar learned this, he said: "That scoundrel Atahuallpa! Does he not know that all this gold and silver which he would give to the Christians is rightfully mine? I myself shall give it to them; then they will kill Atahuallpa."

Atahuallpa's captain-general secretly sent him a message to inform him of what Huáscar had said. Atahuallpa determined to carry out a clever stratagem. When the Marquis invited Atahuallpa to dine, as it was his custom to do, the Indian pretended to be weeping in deep affliction. Learning of this, the Marquis went to find out why. When he asked, Atahuallpa weepingly refused to tell. Finally the Marquis ordered him to speak out.

Atahuallpa replied: "I am in despair because you are about to kill me!"

The Marquis bade the Indian tell him his trouble, promising him he would not be slain.

Atahuallpa finally said: "Lord, you ordered me not to have my brother Huáscar killed, threatening to kill me if it were done. My captains, without knowing of your orders, have slain him, and for this reason I am afraid you will now kill me."

The Marquis, not realizing the trick, asked, "Is Huáscar in very truth dead?"
Atahuallpa said that it was so.

The Marquis reassured him, and told him to be without fear. Since Huáscar had been slain without his knowledge Atahuallpa would come to no harm, nor would he be put to death.

Then, being assured of his life, Atahuallpa quickly sent a messenger to his captains with orders that his brother be slain at once; and so Huáscar was killed and it is said that his body was hurled into a river.

The Marquis kept Atahuallpa prisoner, awaiting the time when the promised treasure should be assembled. He was also waiting for more Spaniards to come to Peru, because he did not dare to press on further with only those he had.

Atahuallpa advised the Marquis that in order to gather the treasure more speedily, it would be necessary to send for the priests who had charge of the treasury of Pachacámac. The Inca sent for these priests, and when they were brought to him he had them held as prisoners.

Atahuallpa also asked that two Spaniards be sent to Cuzco to hasten the bringing of the treasure. The Marquis at once agreed to this, sending two of his men with one of Atahuallpa's Indians to guide them in safety and to give orders that everything they asked for should be yielded.

The Marquis then determined to send his brother Hernando, with fifty horsemen, to Pachacámac.

When Hernando and the men were in readiness, Atahuallpa ordered that the priests of Pachacámac be summoned, and there, in the presence of the Marquis and his brother, he spoke to them saying: "Go with this brother of the Marquis and give to him all the treasure of Pachacámac, your idol, for that Pachacámac of yours is no god, and even if he is, collect the treasure nevertheless."

The Marquis, on learning what Atahuallpa had said, asked him why he claimed that Pachacámac was not a god, since all the Indians held him to be so.

Atahuallpa replied: "Because Pachacámac is a liar."

The Marquis asked him in what respect he had been a liar.

Atahuallpa replied: "You should know, lord, that when my father was sick in Quito, he sent to ask Pachacámac what should be done for his health. Pachacámac commanded that he be taken out into the sun. And when he was taken out, my father died. Then Huáscar, my brother, asked Pachacámac who would win, he or I. Pachacámac said that Huáscar would win, and actually I won. When you came, I sent to ask him who was destined to conquer, you or I, and he sent to tell me that I would. Actually you conquered. Therefore he is a liar, and is no god."

The Marquis said that he, Atahuallpa, knew much.

Atahuallpa replied that shopkeepers know much.

Hernando Pizarro set forth with the guardians of the Idol Pachacámac. But when he arrived he found that most of the treasure had been carried off and hidden by the natives. Out of what remained he sent some two hundred pesos back. After Hernando and the two Spaniards returned to Cajamarca, we received news that Don Diego de Almagro, having heard of the greatness of Peru, was coming from Panama with reinforcements of more than one hundred men.

When Almagro and the troops arrived, Atahuallpa was disturbed because he now suspected that he was going to die. As he was a canny Indian, Atahuallpa had formed a great friendship with Hernando Pizarro, who had promised him that he would not consent to his death. But the Marquis had sent Hernando to Spain with His Majesty's share of the treasure. Atahuallpa wept, saying he would now surely be killed, because Hernando was gone away and because the treasure was being distributed.

Each member of the cavalry was allotted eight thousand pesos and each member of the infantry was given four thousand pesos. The treasure was distributed according to the service of each man and the quality of his horse. But Almagro disagreed violently with this system of distribution, claiming that he and his companion Pizarro were each entitled to half of the treasure and that each of Pizarro's men should get only one thousand, or at most two thousand pesos.

But the Marquis did not allow anyone to be robbed of what he merited. For the treasure had been ordered for all the Spaniards who entered Cajamarca and took part in the capture of Atahuallpa. And to Almagro's men nothing was given.

On account of this, there was a great outburst among the officials of the King who had come with Almagro, for these officials said that the treasure of Peru was limitless and that if Atahuallpa's declaration that the treasure was only for the Spaniards who had been in Cajamarca was kept they would never get anything. The officials and Almagro agreed, therefore, that Atahuallpa should die, and that once he was dead, his sworn proclamation about the treasure would be void. These newcomers said to the Marquis that it was not fitting that Atahuallpa should live, for if he ever escaped, His Majesty would lose the land and all the Spaniards in Peru would be slain.

But the Marquis did not wish to kill Atahuallpa. Seeing this, the officials made many demands upon him, setting the service of His Majesty above all.

While matters were thus, one of the interpreters, called Felipillo, became enamored of a wife of Atahuallpa's and in order to win her told the Marquis that Atahuallpa was having a great assemblage of troops collected to fall upon the Spaniards and kill them. The Marquis summoned Atahuallpa's captain-general and inquired about these troops. Atahuallpa's general denied that there was such an army. But Felipillo treacherously translated the words to mean their very opposite. Still the Marquis had no wish to kill Atahuallpa. So he sent Soto to find out if any troops were being assembled.

Almagro and the officials, seeing the departure of Soto, hastened to the Marquis and, as the interpreter on his part aided them with his slyness, they in time convinced Don Francisco that Atahuallpa should die.

Against his will the Marquis sentenced Atahuallpa to death, commanding that he should be executed and that his body should be burned.

Atahuallpa wept, and he besought them not to kill him, saying that there was not an Indian in the land who would stir without his command, and what had the Spaniards to fear, holding him a prisoner? If they were doing this for gold or silver, the Inca said he would give them twice as much as he had already ordered.

I saw the Marquis weep with sorrow at not being able to grant Atahuallpa his life. But he certainly feared danger if Atahuallpa should escape.

This Atahuallpa was an Indian of fine person, of medium size, beautiful of face and grave, a man much feared by his people. When the Spaniards took Atahuallpa out to kill him, all the natives who were in the plaza prostrated themselves upon the ground, letting themselves fall like drunken men.

The priest Fray Vicente de Valverde preached to the Inca, bidding him to become a Christian. Atahuallpa asked if they would burn him should he become a Christian, and they told him no. He then agreed to be baptized. So Fray Vicente baptized him and they executed him. And on another day they buried him in Cajamarca.

When Atahuallpa was killed, a number of troops, one of his sisters, and several other Indian women were killed so that they could go to the other world to serve him.

Two other sisters remained, and they went about chanting great lamentations and singing accounts of the deeds of Atahuallpa. They asked me to let them go into the room where the Inca had been imprisoned. Once inside the room they

began to call to Atahuallpa, seeking for him very gently in corners. I asked them what they were seeking, and they told me they were looking for their lord. I disillusioned them, and told them that the dead do not come back.

Soon after these events, Soto returned to report that he had not seen any Indian troops. On account of this, the Marquis sorrowed even more deeply for having killed Atahuallpa.

After the death of Atahuallpa, the Marquis raised up Inca Tubalipa as King. This Indian was a son of Huaina Cápac and a brother of Huáscar. He was crowned according to the laws of the Indians.

The Marquis then commanded that all the Spaniards make ready to march throughout the land, saying that thenceforward all the treasure which should be found would be for all.

This gave great pleasure to those who came with Almagro.

We soon arrived at the valley of Xauxa, where the Marquis halted us for some days in order that the troops might rest. He established a settlement here, the second village founded by the Spaniards in Peru.

While we were stopping in this place, we were informed that Tubalipa had died of a slow-acting poison which had been put into his *chincha* (a beer) by Challichuchima, a general of Atahuallpa's.

After resting, the Marquis commanded that the troops who were to go to Cuzco should set forth from Xauxa. In Cuzco so many Indians came to see us that the fields were covered with them.

I shall now give an account of what was in this city of Cuzco when we entered it. There were storehouses filled to capacity with bars of copper from the mines, wooden vessels, and plates of gold and silver. The Indians apparently did not value objects of gold and silver very highly, for had they done so they would have hidden them better.

Among the most notable pieces that we discovered were twelve awnings of gold and silver, pitchers half of pottery and half of gold, and a figure of gold which the Indians said represented the first Inca who conquered this land.

However, some Indian soldiers secretly carried much of the Incas' treasure to a secluded spot. Fifty or one hundred of them buried the treasure and covered it over well. Then they hanged themselves from certain remote trees. They slew themselves without leaving one alive. It will be a miracle if this treasure is ever found.

PART IV

From Garcilaso de la Vega

ROYAL ROADS

The Inca kings divided their empire into four parts. They placed the city of Cuzco in the center, for in the language of the Incas the word *cuzco* means "a navel." The city's name is therefore very appropriate, for the whole of Peru is long and narrow, like a human body, and Cuzco is almost in the middle.

The Incas built royal roads which led from Cuzco to the four corners of the empire. The remains of two magnificent roads, which extended throughout Peru from north to south, can still be seen. One of them passes along the coast, and the other transverses the mountains inland. Historians speak of these works with admiration, but all their praise falls short of the grandeur of the achievement.

The two roads cover a distance of fifteen hundred miles, in a country where there are great ascents and descents. On the highest parts of the roads are large platforms with masonry steps where those who carried the royal litter rested themselves, and where the Inca often stopped to enjoy the view. In some places, one can see for hundreds of miles. The mountain peaks appear to reach the heavens, while the valleys and ravines are so deep that they seem to approach the center of the earth.

In the valleys of the coast and in the vast sandy deserts, the tall poles which served as guides to prevent travelers from losing their way can still be seen along the road sites.

RUNNERS AND THE MESSAGES THEY CARRIED

The Incas had runners posted along their roads whose duty it was to carry the king's orders, and to bring important news to Cuzco from nearby and distant provinces of the empire. Four to six swift Indian lads were stationed in huts at intervals of three quarters of a mile, because that was the distance that an Indian could run at full speed without getting tired.

Two huts were built at each station to protect the runners from the weather. The huts were always placed on high ground so that they could be seen from the opposite side of the road. The runners in the two huts alternated in carrying the dispatches. Those in one hut watched the road in one direction, and those in the other watched in the opposite direction, so that they could see the messengers before they arrived at the stations, and thus be ready to take the dispatch. Some of the messages which the runners carried were verbal, because the Indians of Peru could not write. The words were curt and to the point, so that they would not be misunderstood or forgotten.

As soon as he was within hearing of the station, the runner shouted out his message, repeating it two, three, or four times until it was understood. If this failed, he waited until he arrived and delivered it more formally. Thus the dispatch was passed from one runner to the next until it reached its destination.

QUIPUS

Other dispatches were carried by knotted strings of different colors. The strings were closely woven in three or four strands, and were attached to a thicker cord, from which they hung in the manner of a fringe. The Indians called these knotted strings *quipus*, which means "to knot" or "a knot," so that the word serves as both a verb and a noun. The thing to which a string referred was understood by its color: for instance, a yellow string referred to gold, a white one to silver, and a red one to soldiers. The knots indicated units: tens, hundreds, thousands, and tens of thousands. The Incas kept records of everything in their kingdom relating to numbers with the knots, and used them to add and multiply.

ASTRONOMY

The Incas had some knowledge of astronomy. They watched the moon increase and wane but they did not know what caused this occurrence. After the moon was lost to sight they did not see it for three days, and they called this the death of the moon.

They regarded the sun with wonder. At one season it seemed to approach, giving them much heat, and at another season it seemed more distant from them, and the days were cooler. Sometimes the days were shorter than the nights, sometimes they were longer, and at certain times the days and nights were of equal length.

The Incas understood that the course of the sun's movements was completed in a single year. They regulated their season for sowing by the solar year, and divided one year from another.

They reckoned the months from one new moon to another. They gave a special name to each month, but they did not have names for the days of the month.

They observed the eclipses of the sun and of the moon, but they did not understand their cause. When a solar eclipse occurred, they said that the sun was enraged at some offense that had been committed against it, for it looked disturbed like the face of an angry man, and they prophesied that some heavy chastisement was approaching.

When a lunar eclipse took place, seeing the moon become dark, they thought that she was ill. When the moon was completely eclipsed, they believed that she was dead and would fall from the sky and kill everyone beneath, and that the end of the world would come. When such an eclipse began, they were in great terror, and sounded trumpets, horns, and drums, and all the other instruments they possessed, making a loud noise. They tied up all the dogs and gave them many blows to make them call to the moon; for they believed that the moon was fond of dogs, and they hoped that when the moon heard the dogs cry she would be sorry for them and awake from the sleep caused by sickness.

They also told the children to cry aloud, calling upon *Mama Quilla*, which means "Mother Moon," and beseeching her not to die and so cause them all to perish.

When the sun set, seeing it sink into the sea, they said that on entering the water it dried up a great portion of the sea by its fire and heat; and, like a swimmer, made a great dive under the earth, to rise the next day in the east. But they said nothing touching the setting of the moon or of the stars.

The Incas took account of only three planets, and they did not know what caused their movements. They did not know of the other planets.

CEREMONIES TO DRIVE OUT EVIL

One of the great and solemn ceremonies which the Inca kings celebrated in their court was intended as a means of banishing all disease and trouble from the city of Cuzco and its vicinity. The high priest performed the ceremonies.

As soon as the Sun rose, all the people worshiped him. When the act of worship was completed, an Inca of the blood royal came forth from the fortress at Sacsahuaman richly dressed as a messenger of the Sun with his mantle girded round his body and a lance in his hand. The lance was adorned with feathers of many colors and fastened with rings of gold.

The Indian ran down the hill from the fortress, brandishing his lance, until he reached the center of the great square where there were four other Incas of the blood royal, each with a lance in his hand and his mantle girded up. The runner touched with his lance the lances of the other four, and told them that the Sun had ordered them as his messengers to drive the evils from the city.

The four Incas then separated, running down the four royal roads which lead out of Cuzco. While they ran, all the inhabitants came to the doors of their house and, with great shouts of joy, shook the clothes they had on, as if they were shaking off dust. They then passed their hands over their heads, faces, arms, and legs, as if in the act of washing.

They did these things to drive the evils out of their houses, so that the messengers of the Sun might banish them from Cuzco.

DOMESTIC ANIMALS

There are two kinds of domestic animals in Peru, one larger than the other. The Indians call them *llama*.

The larger ones are called *huánucu-llama*. These animals are of all colors, like the horses in Spain. They resemble a camel without the hump, and are about one-third the size of a camel. Their necks are long and graceful.

The Indians rub the skins of the llamas with grease until they are pliable and like dressed leather, and use them for the soles of their shoes.

The llamas are also useful for carrying goods. Their rate of speed is about nine miles a day, for they are not beasts that will do much work. They cannot be persuaded to change their fixed pace, for they will become tired if they are urged, and presently lie down. If this happens, nothing will induce them to rise, even if their load is taken off. When an attempt is made to raise them, they defend themselves by spitting in the face of the nearest man. One then has to flay them, for there is nothing else to be done.

The llamas cost their owners nothing in food, lodging, shoeing, harnesses, pack saddles, girths, straps, or other things that are usually needed for beasts. On arriving at their resting place, they are unloaded and turned adrift to browse on such pasture as they can find, and thus they maintain themselves without being given either grain or straw. They do not require shoeing because their hoofs are fleshy and not horny. They do not require pack saddles or harnesses of any kind, for they have such thick wool that the load can be placed upon it, if the packer takes care to distribute the load equally, and prevents it from touching the animal's spine.

The smaller kind is called *paco-llama*, and there is not as much to say about it, as it is not useful for carrying loads. However, the wool of this animal is excellent and very long. The Indians make three kinds of cloth from the wool, and color it with beautiful dyes which never fade, and which they know well how to apply.

To keep track of their multitude of llamas the Incas divided them according to their colors. If a llama was born a different color from its parents, it was removed to a flock of its own color as soon as it was raised. By means of their knots the Indians kept an account of the llamas with great ease, as the threads were dyed the same color as the flocks to which they referred.

WILD ANIMALS AND BIRDS OF PREY

There is also a wild sheep called the *vicuña* in Peru. It is a small and delicate animal with much fine wool. The vicuña stands higher than the largest goat. Its wool is a very clear chestnut color. These animals are very swift, and no greyhound can come near them. They browse on very lofty deserts.

Lions are met with in Peru, though they are not so large or so fierce as those in Africa. The Indians call them *puma*.

There are many monkeys, large and small.

Very large birds are found which may be classified as birds of prey. The Spaniards call them *condors*. They are fifteen to sixteen feet long from the tip of one wing to the tip of the other. Their claws are like those of a chicken, and their beaks are strong enough to break through the hide of a cow. Two condors will attack a cow and a bull and eat them.

DAILY WORK

The Incas had no tailors, shoemakers, nor hosiers. The women looked after the clothing belonging to the house, and the men took care of the shoes. They all knew how to make sandals.

In the work of the field, men and women generally helped one another. But in some provinces, a great distance from Cuzco, the women went to work in the fields and the men stayed at home to spin and weave.

The Indian women were so fond of work and such enemies to wasting even the shortest space of time that even in going from their villages to the city, or in passing from one house to another on necessary business, they took with them the materials for spinning and weaving.

DECORATION OF TEMPLES AND PALACES

The Incas possessed gold, silver, and precious stones in great quantities, but these were not considered to be treasure, and buying and selling with gold and silver were unknown. They were valued for their beauty and splendor alone, and were used to adorn the palaces and temples of the Inca kings.

The decoration of these buildings was grand and magnificent. The Indians plated the temples of the Sun and the royal palaces with gold. They left recesses in the walls and put in them many gold and silver figures of men and women, and of animals such as lions, tigers, bears, foxes, dogs, cats, deer, and llamas, all worked in imitation of nature. They made birds of all kinds; some sitting on branches, others flying and sucking honey from the flowers.

Attached to the royal palaces were gardens and orchards in which were planted all the beautiful trees and sweet flowers in Peru.

The Incas also placed flowers of gold and silver in these gardens. Some were depicted just beginning to sprout; others were shown half-grown, and others at maturity.

In the temple of the Sun at Cuzco there was a garden of gold and silver containing many herbs and flowers, small plants, trees, and large and small animals, both wild and domestic. There was also a large field of maize, and an orchard of trees with their fruit.

The king Inca usually sat on a stool of solid gold, which was placed on a golden platform. All the cups for the service of the king were of gold and silver and some were placed in each royal lodging for his use when traveling.

GOLD AND SILVER

Spain is a good witness of the wealth that has been obtained from Peru in gold and silver. For the last twenty-five years, the Spanish have annually collected twelve to thirteen millions of pesos in these metals.

Gold is found in all parts of Peru, though in some provinces it is more abundant than in others. It is found on the surface of the land and also in the rivers and streams, and is obtained from these places by washing the earth and sand. The Spaniards call that which is obtained by washing gold-dust, because it comes out like filings. Occasionally large nuggets are found.

Silver is obtained with more trouble than gold, and is prepared and purified at greater cost. There are mines of silver in many parts of Peru, but none have been found which equal those of Potocsi, which were discovered and registered in the year 1545, fourteen years after the Spaniards entered the land. The hill where the mines are is in the form of a sugar loaf, rising out of a plain, and is three miles round. It is more than three quarters of a mile high, and is beautiful to look upon.

BUILDING IN STONE

The Incas built grand edifices: fortresses, temples, palaces, storehouses, and other works.

The walls of their houses and temples were made of wonderfully cut masonry. The stones were placed so exactly against each other that there was no need of mortar, and the buildings were so well constructed that they would have endured for many ages if they had not been destroyed by the Spaniards.

One of the grandest and most superb structures built by the Incas was the fortress of Cuzco. The multitude of enormous stones which make up the ruins of the fortress arouses wonder as to how they could have been cut from the quarries in the area, for the Incas had neither iron nor steel for cutting.

It was an awesome task to transport the stones from the quarries, as the Indians did not have bullocks or carts. The stones were drawn by sheer manual force—hauled by stout cables over steep mountain roads. Many were brought from thirty or forty miles away.

The Indians had no squares or rulers to put on top of the stones to see if they were correctly set for receiving others. Moreover, they had no engines for lifting and lowering them. Yet the stones were so perfectly adjusted that the point of a knife could scarcely be inserted between them.

The Incas also constructed a fortress on a lofty hill north of Cuzco called Sacsahuanaman. They erected a beautifully worked stone wall on all sides but the one facing the city, where the hill is almost perpendicular.

In building this fortress, the Incas displayed all their knowledge, desiring that it should excel in workmanship and splendor all those that had been erected before it, and be their trophy of trophies.

Soon after the fortress was finished, the Spaniards put an end to other great works which were in the course of construction.